MY ALLAH SERIES
ALLAH IS THE MOST WISE

KISA KIDS PUBLICATIONS

AL-KISA
FOUNDATION
WWW.KISAKIDS.ORG

PARENTS' CORNER

وَاللَّـهُ عَلِيمٌ حَكِيمٌ

And Allāh is All-Knowing, All-Wise
(Sūrat an-Nisā, Verse 26)

Dear Parents/Guardians,

It is possible that older children who defiantly question Islām may have ideological problems that stem from their lack of understanding and belief in Allāh's wisdom. Their belief in Allāh's wisdom may be weak and therefore they do not trust Him to do what is best for them, and as a result, they have difficulty following Allāh's orders.

It is vital and of utmost importance that parents strengthen the understanding of Allāh's wisdom in young children. It is important to continuously remind them that Allāh created us and takes care of us; He wants us to become good Muslims, get closer to Him, and go to Jannah. Through these reminders, children will innately strengthen their love and trust in Allāh deep in their hearts. Additionally, it is very important for parents to keep reminding themselves and their children that Allāh is the Most Knowledgeable and always knows what is best for us, even though we might not always understand why.

If this understanding is strengthened in our children at a young age, inshāAllāh they will grow up to ask questions about their dīn in a positive manner, so that they can understand it better. They will become more confident and content with fulfilling their duties, such as salāh, ḥijāb, and fasting, inshāAllāh.

We hope that *Allah is the Most Wise* will encourage your children to ponder upon Allāh's wisdom and miracles and realize that He truly is the All-Wise.

With Duʻas,
Kisa Kids Publications

When you look at a tall building,
you know the builder must be very smart.
He must be an expert and know all about
its different parts.

Have you ever seen how tall buildings are made?

When you see a beautiful piece of art,
you know the artist must be very smart.

Who gave painters the hands they paint with?

4

When you see an airplane flying high above the trees,
you know the clever engineer knows a lot about machines.

Where would you go in an airplane?

5

When you see a farmer busy with his planting,
you realize he must know a lot about farming.

What are some fruits a farmer grows?

But who made the birds, the trees, and the sun?
Of course Allah, the Mighty, the One.
Everywhere I turn and look with my two eyes,
I try to see how Allah is the Most Wise.

What are some other things Allah has created so perfectly?

When I look in the mirror, I see how Allah made me carefully.
If my eyes were under my feet, how would I be able to see?
Allah placed my hands, legs, and eyes exactly where they should be.
Thinking of every detail, He's the Most Wise, the al-Hakeem!

What would happen if your eyes were not on your head, but were on your hands and feet instead?

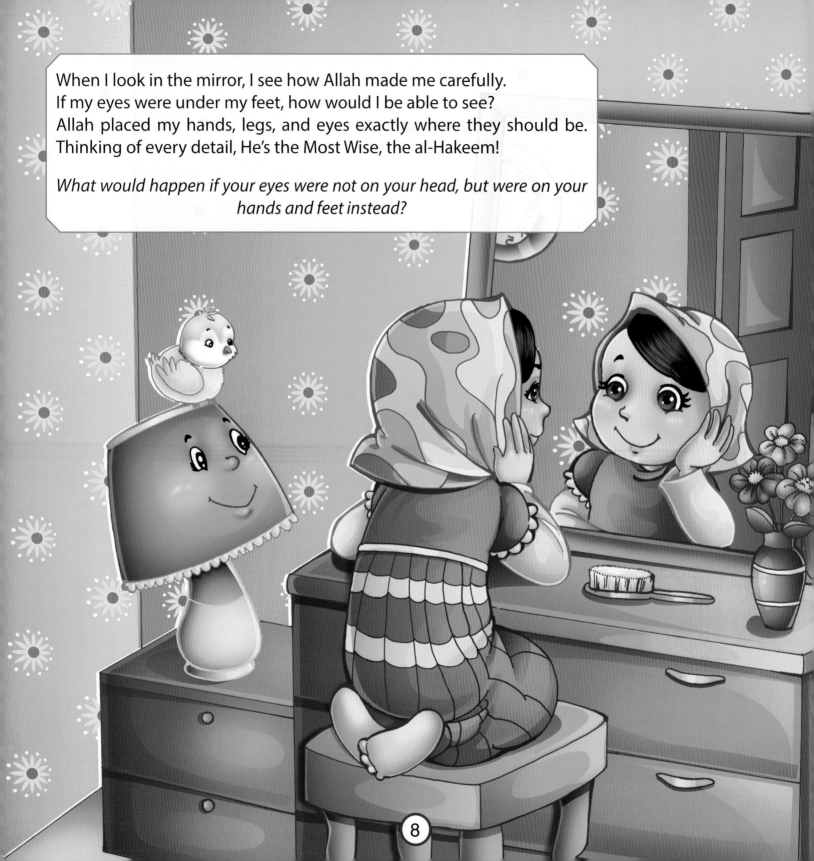

Allah gave me fingers to eat spaghetti and rice. Allah knows everything, and is the Most Wise!

Try picking up something without your thumb, only using 4 fingers. What happens?

Allah gave me teeth to eat my meals and my snacks.
The front teeth bite the food, and it gets chewed in the back.
This way, I can eat apples, chicken, and pies.
Allah knows everything, He is the Most Wise!

What are some things you eat using your teeth?

Allah gave me eyebrows so when I sweat,
it doesn't drip and hurt my eyes.
Allah knows everything, He is the most Wise!

What games make you sweat?

Look at the stork with its extra long beak.
It can catch fish from the water, even when it's deep!
The more I look, the more I see,
How Allah made the world so perfectly!

What are some other amazing and perfect things Allah created?